SE

from the Inside-Out

"Anybody can be great, because anybody can serve. You don't have to have a college degree to serve. You don't have to make your verb and subject agree to serve.

You only need a heart full of grace. A soul generated by love."

Dr. Martin Luther King Jr.

SERVICE

from the Inside-Out

A Simple Guide for
Wowing the Customer,
Making a Difference and Loving Life

Darren J. Bagshaw

INSIDE-OUT
TRAINING AND DEVELOPMENT

SERVICE FROM THE INSIDE-OUT

 For information address Inside-Out Training & Development P.O. Box #43096 1221 Canyon Meadows Drive S.E. Calgary, Alberta, Canada T2J 7A7

http://www.insideouttraining.com

First printed in paperback by Inside-Out Training & Development: 2001

Canadian Cataloguing in Publication Data

Bagshaw, Darren James, 1967-
Service from the Inside-Out: A Simple Guide for Wowing the Customer, Making a difference and Loving Life

1st edition

ISBN 0-9686878-1-4
1. Business 2. Psychology/ Self-help

Printed and Bound in Canada

To my wonderful family.
Lipi, you are the passion of my life.
Kennedy, Christian and Alisha
you are my inspiration.

I'd like to thank...

Lipi, my amazing wife, partner and soul mate for her undying support. The greatest joy of my life is building our family together.

My father, Jim, for teaching me anything is possible and to my mother, Karen, who showed me the power of unconditional love and support. Michael and Kimberly you're the greatest. Sham and Nazma for always treating me as your own son.

Tad Hargrave for your invaluable insights into this book and your friendship. Guy Gehmlich, you da' man. Brandon Bays for letting your light shine. Robin Sharma for always sharing your wisdom. Paul, Bruce and Greg, thank you for your support.

Thank you to all of the ARA team and graduates who have been such a special part of my journey.

To all of our Inside-Out clients who believe that the best way to increase the bottom line is to help increase their peoples' quality of life.

Lyle Krause for your outstanding production efforts on this and all the Inside-Out projects.

I am grateful to the modern masters, Wayne Dyer, Anthony Robbins, Deepak Chopra, Stephen Covey and Oprah Winfrey who have lighted the path for us all to follow. The ancient masters whose wisdom still guides us today and Jesus, for giving me the strength to follow my dreams.

Contents

"What you need to do may seem insignificant, but it is very significant that you do it."

Mahatma Gandhi

Introduction

THE MOMENT OF TRUTH

Imagine. You have just spent three years as a leader of a team. You have worked your tail off to make this a world-class team. Your priority was always to build up your people and add value to the community. Your sole objective was to increase the quality of life for your team and the customers your team served. You were amazing. You pulled off miracles that no one thought would be possible.

Now imagine, after three years, a member of your team betrays you. The customers who you have worked so hard to serve turn against you. Even your most loyal VPs aren't there when you need them most. How would you feel? Angry? Frustrated? Betrayed? Unappreciated? How would you lash out? Would you determine to get your revenge by going to a competitor? Would you turn your back on those would had betrayed you?

Now imagine the last day in the life of Jesus Christ. The utter humiliation. The intense pain. His own people had turned against him. It is nearly impossible to imagine the anguish that any one of us would feel as nails pierced our skin and attached us to a wooden cross to be crucified because of who we were, by the very people we had devoted our lives to helping. Yet in that moment, a moment of truth, in unbearable pain, Jesus exclaimed "Forgive them father, they know not what they do".

It is in our moments of truth that our life is defined. This is what has made people like Gandhi, Nelson Mandela, Mother Teresa, J.F.K. and Martin Luther King Jr. icons of what the human spirit is capable of. They made the most of their moments of truth. It is not just the great climatic moments of our lives, like Mel Gibson's character William Wallace in the epic BraveHeart who beaten and broken from the interrogators tortures yells "*freedom*" with his dieing breathe, it is the every day moments that create our living legacy that becomes who we are. A moment of truth is any moment when who we really are, or more importantly, who we are striving to become, is put to the test.

A moment of truth is when we are faced with a customer who is *wrong* and we need to decide are we going to be of service and honor their greatness or are we going to be *right*. It is when our child expresses their sense of independence and individuality and in the moment we can either create obedience, teaching them to blindly follow authority, or we can allow that child to express themselves and support their self-esteem, which creates leaders. That is a moment of truth.

As the level of Competition continues to increase, Excellence is no longer the standard.

In every area of life, the level of competition continues to increase. The global economy and the advent of e-commerce has created an environment that can see market leaders change over night and competition come out of nowhere and blind side us before we have a chance to react.

With merger mania and technological advancements the new question is …is your job or organization redundant?

In our families we have to compete for our children's attention against popular culture. Music, peers, television and of course, the Internet. The Internet with all its wonderful advantages has allowed the world into our homes. The one place we felt our children would be safe from the outside world. The underbelly of society can now stock our children in chat rooms by masquerading as something they are not.

The world has changed radically in the twenty years since the breakthrough book "in Search of Excellence" raised the bar for the acceptable standard. In today's environment, excellence is no longer enough. Think about it in your own business. What is the minimum your customers expect from you? Good? I don't think so. What happens when consumers only receive a good value for their investment of time, energy or capital? They are looking for a better value. We are living in a transactional age. The consumer is more educated than ever before.

Excellence is the minimum Standard

What is great service? I'm sure you can come up with a whole list of words that describe what great service is. Words like fast, courteous, added value and guaranteed. If I asked you to go out and find examples of great service, there is no doubt you could find them, although it may take you a while. We all know it when we experience it. And we certainly know it when we don't.

The current model in the business world is that in order for an organization to provide great service on a consistent basis the organization must create a culture to support it. They must have the policies in place with the systems to support it. They must have the managers to ensure the systems are implemented and motivate the frontline personnel to actually use them. They must give the frontline staff increasing levels of external motivation to meet the rapid growth in the global economy. While this certainly may help, this does not guarantee the customer will receive even adequate service.

Outstanding

Great service is not a result of a huge organizational machine cranking out this intangible product called service. **It is the result of a single individual, and often a team of individuals, who understand the joy of adding value to their customers.**

I am not just taking about people in a traditional customer service role. I am talking about everyone who is in a position to add value to someone or something else (for all you environmentalists). This ranges from CEO's to cashiers. From sales people, to tow truck drivers, to systems analysts. Parents, teachers, doctors, anyone who is in the position to make an impact.

What is Service?

True Service means to give unconditionally. To give of your time, energy, talents, money and even emotions without expectation of something in return. To give joyfully and perhaps even without the recipient's knowledge. Mother Teresa defined service best when she said, " Let no one come to you with out leaving better and happier."

The definition we will use for great service is to ***consistently have the customer leaving the transaction/ interaction feeling better than before it began.***

Service is one of life's greatest joys. Service is the key ingredient that holds the company/ customer relationship in place. For that matter, it's the mortar in any relationship.

Service is not a list of steps to follow when dealing with a customer or a magic switch we turn on when they walk in the door, call us on the phone or send an E-mail. It's not exclusive to Christmas. Service is not only about giving money to a Sunday afternoon infomercial on starving children because you feel guilty. It is definitely not only something that you gave at the office.

Service is a part of every aspect of life. As Bob Dylan sang about "You gotta serve somebody". It is the choice of who you are going to serve that makes all the difference. Choosing to serve yourself, your job or money leads you down an endless path of meaningless frustration. On the other hand, choosing to serve your customers, your family, your community brings with it unlimited rewards.

Service is a way of life. In fact, it is the purpose to life. The lives that have the most meaning and the greatest satisfaction are the lives lived in service. Now don't worry, I'm not suggesting you give up all your earthly possessions and move to a third world country. Service can show up in many different forms. From a mother taking care of her child to Ted Turner donating 1 Billion dollars to the UN. From a volunteer at a soup kitchen to a sales person helping her customer to find the right product for his needs.

One is not better than the other. They are just different. We all arrive in this lifetime with a unique set of skills and talents. It is our job to discover what they are and use them to be of service to the occupants of this planet.

Nothing is more rewarding than the feeling we get when we genuinely give to someone else. I know you have experienced it. The time you found the perfect gift or when you went the extra mile for that difficult customer. Or, maybe, it was as simple as smiling at a stranger and you could tell it made their day.

Mom & Dad

How does this apply to parents? Exactly the same. Great service as parents means being a living example of the values and principles that we want our children to grow up with. It means to nurture that child and making self-esteem the number #1 priority.

If parents do not give great service to their children, what happens? Don't the children suffer? When they are young, of course they do. However, we hear all the time about children who realize that as adults they are responsible for their own lives and have overcome all kinds of unimaginable upbringings to become well-adjusted, happy adults. The real loser is the parent. Their time spent with their children will be tiresome and unfulfilled. As their children grow and leave home they have to live with the guilt and sorrow of their unfulfilled potential as parents. And, very likely, they will have little if any real relationship with their children.

On the other hand, the parent who realizes there is no role more important than that of a parent will reap all the rewards parenthood has to offer. Their time with their children is filled with joy and fulfillment. As their children grow and leave home, they will have a relationship based on mutual respect, understanding and, of course, love. Even if they do not have an ongoing relationship with their children, they can live with the satisfaction they did the best they could.

As hopefully you can see, the greatest win comes to those who have chosen a life of Service.

Why this Book?

This book is not about thank you cards or follow-up phone calls or smiling and using a person's name. Those are the mechanics of service. Almost everyone understands the basics of giving great service. *Yet very few of us do them consistently.*

This book is about what prevents people from doing the basics, and more importantly, how to break through the barriers that will allow you to do them on a consistent basis. ***Service from the Inside-Out is designed to be an easy to use guide*** *filled with ideas you can put into action immediately to create a constantly increasing quality of life.*

This is a book for those organizations that understand that it is the individual who make the greatest impact on their "Customer Service Machines".

In the end, Service from the Inside-Out, is based on the belief that a single motivated individual can have a profound, lasting effect on the people they come in contact with. *A single candle can penetrate even the darkest night.*

How to use this book

The Service from the Inside-Out is designed to be used as a guide to delivering outstanding service on a consistent basis, while increasing your quality of life.

1. ***Read it***. This is the key to getting value from

any book. Whether you made the conscious decision to buy it or it somehow ended up in your hands, you have it for a reason. There is only one way to find out what the reason is; read it. You can read it as a traditional book, from cover to cover, or you can jump around from section to section. I have broken it down into bite size chunks that you can read in a few minutes get a new idea or skill, and then go off and use it.

2. ***Highlight key points.*** Everyone is different. What you may find as a destiny-shaping concept, someone else may just skim over. And vice versa. Use a highlighter and mark the key passages that have an impact on you or skills you want to develop. Reading a book this way has two benefits;
    A. You are more focused on finding the value for yourself.
    B. It is easier to go back through the book and pull out the key concepts.

3. ***Make Notes.*** Imagine you are going to get tested on the material in this book (actually, you are, Life is the test). There is space at the end of the chapters and in the margin, make good use of it.

4. ***Try it, then decide.*** This book is filled with lots of ideas, some you will be familiar with, some you won't. They all have tremendous value to offer you. However don't take my word for it, try them for yourself. Whether you are really ex-

cited about the idea or less than thrilled, give them a good ten days. If after ten days you find they have no value for you, then punt them. If they have value, keep them and keep practicing.

5. ***Have Fun!*** We learn best when we are having fun. As you will discover, having fun is a choice.

One final thought before we begin:

The Individual who takes
Personal Responsibility
for delivering
Outstanding Service
and understands that
Emotional Certainty
Is a Choice,
Not a Reward,
is the individual who will
Thrive
in our
ever-changing world.

Enjoy.

Chapter 1
THE CHALLENGE

It's a bright sunny day and you are enjoying a latte at your favorite coffee shop patio. As the conversation winds down your best friend realizes that she has forgotten her wallet and asks to borrow $5.

The challenge is that you are running a little short yourself. You don't have $5 to give to her. At least if you had the $5 you would have a choice. You can lend the money or not lend the money. However, because you *do not have it,* you cannot share it.

This story illustrates the most important concept to provide outstanding service in today's marketplace. You can only give what you have.

Great Service Anyone?

When was the last time you truly had great service? I mean the kind that wows you so much it puts a smile on your face for the whole day because you can hardly believe it.

It seems funny, practically every company out there has "Service First", "Superior Service" or "Customers First" as part of their market positioning, yet its hard to find anyone who experiences great service on a regular basis.

Virtually every company and organization in the market place has identified service as the key competitive advantage. They have invested huge amounts of capital, time and energy to create the policies and systems necessary to deliver consistently great service. Most of these companies have even gone the step further and trained their people how to deliver great service, especially when there is a "customer service challenge".

So, when it comes to service, today's workforce knows what to do and even how to do it, yet the experience of truly outstanding service is a truly rare occurrence.

Stuff Happens

I had just worked all weekend finishing an important proposal. It was Monday morning and it had to get to LA from my home office in Calgary, Alberta by noon the next day. I called an internationally recognized courier that guaranteed overnight delivery. I talked to one of their operators and arranged for the pick -up. I was told the driver would be by before 8 p.m. At about 7 p.m. I was getting a little concerned so I called again to see how things were coming along.

The "indifferent" operator informed me that the computer system had crashed and they had lost my order. Okay, I thought, these kinds of challenges happen. It's not her fault. So I inquired as to what we can do about getting my package there on time. There was no way they could get my package there on time. So I thought that all I needed to do was to get a letter from the courier outlining that the proposal would have been there on time if they had not missed the pick-up. To file a complaint I would have to put my name on a list and the Customer Service person would call me within 48 hours.

After I pointed out to her their overnight guarantee, she agreed to have the package picked up the next day and delivered for free.

The next day the driver showed up to get the package, however he had no idea it was to be delivered for free. To his credit he just took the package and said he would take care of it when he got back to the warehouse.

On Tuesday, there was no call from the Customer Service person. Nor Wednesday. Nor Thursday. Finally at about 7 p.m. on Thursday I decide to give them a ring.

Once again I was informed they had somehow lost my file in the computer. After a very long discussion, the operator put me through to a Customer Service advisor.

Of course, I was now wondering why we couldn't do this the first time.

The Customer Service Advisor, who I had waited three days to talk to, obviously wasn't thrilled to hear from me. My request was simple. They offered "overnight delivery guaranteed" as did their competitors. All I wanted was a letter stating that my proposal would have been there on time if they had not lost my order.

I was given a long speech about how "impossible" this request was. We finally boiled it down to the fact she did not want to take the time to fill out all of the paper work. Once again, I had to use the leverage of their guarantee to get my letter.

Was this an example of great Service? Of course not. Did the company have the policies in place to "satisfy" my needs? Yes, they did. Were the employees trained on how to "handle" a customer like me? I'm going to guess that at least the Customer Service Advisor was. Do challenges like this happen in business everyday? Most certainly.

So the question is, if the policies are in place to deliver service and the people have been trained on "how to" deliver on these policies, what then is the secret to great service?

Service Happens In A Moment
The Moment of Truth

Service comes down to the state (mood) of the person who is delivering it. Nothing more, nothing less. Whatever state we are in gets transferred to the people we are interacting with. When the Customer Service Advisor picked up the phone, that was a moment of truth. Her state determined the quality of that interaction. Because she chose to be in an average state, she accessed average amounts of her potential and produced less than average service.

Outstanding Service comes when an Individual takes personal responsibility for delivering it.

If you are excited about your job and believe in your product, its that excitement and congruency that is transferred to the client. On the other hand, if you're frustrated with your job and could care less about the product, this also gets transferred to the client.

The better the state the person is in, the better the service they will provide. The poorer the state the less likely they are to deliver satisfactory service. Even if they follow through with the appropriate policies, they are likely to do it in such a way the customer will be less than satisfied.

When we are in a good state, we have greater access to our potential to take action. We are more emotionally flexible and therefore can handle a wider variety of situations.

When we are in a poor state, the funnel to our potential is closed off and we have almost no emotional flexibility. The main focus is just getting through the day, not "How can I serve my customers?".

I'm sure you have had the experience of going to a department store or maybe your neighborhood convenience store and the clerk acted as if they were doing you a favor by taking your money.

The difference between great service and poor service is very much like the difference between being effective and being efficient. When someone is being efficient, they are focused on doing the things right. They spend all of their time doing what they are supposed to do and very little time focusing on getting them done properly. When someone is being effective, they focus on doing the right things. These are the types of people who understand that it is the *state* in which the service is being carried out that makes all the difference.

As an example, there is a chain of grocery stores that requires all of its cashiers to call you by name. When you hand them your credit or debit card, they glance at it and say something like "Thank you for shopping with us, have a nice day Mr. Jones". Great strategy because people like being called by their name. However, here is the difference between efficient and effective.

> ***Efficient:*** *It was a busy evening at the grocery store. The line-up was long and I was in a hurry to get home before the kids went to bed. As I got to the cashier I could tell she was having a long day. She*

your favorite kind. Mine is a Mandarin. What happens when you squeeze the orange? Juice comes out. What happens if you put it on the floor and jump up and down on it? Orange juice comes out. It doesn't matter how you squeeze the orange; orange juice is going to come out, because orange juice is on the inside.

The same is true of people. Whatever "juice" they have on the inside is what comes out when they get squeezed. The idea is to have sweet orange juice pouring out and not sour lemon juice.

What squeezes people? Budgets, deadlines, technology, change, relationships.

If a person is excited about their job, what comes out when they are squeezed? Excitement. Excitement under stress may look more like determination, however it is still a resourceful state. On the other hand, what comes out if the person is stressed about their job? Stress. Stress can manifest itself in many ways. Anger, frustration, depression, none of them resourceful. Definitely not the states associated with great service.

"A good man out of the treasure of his heart bringeth forth that which is good; and an evil man out of the evil treasure of his heart bringeth forth that which is evil: for of the abundance of the heart his mouth speaketh."
Luke 6:45

How did I get so Sour?

As the saying goes, "Garbage in, Garbage out". The feelings we experience, our juice, are created by how we filter what is going on in the world around us.

When we have an effective, efficient filtration system, we are able to process the squeezers for what they really are, valuable information. As we use this information properly we can create resourceful states. The squeezers, the challenges, in life are the key to our growth. Without obstacles to overcome we would wither and die from lack of use. This is evidenced by how quickly some people's health deteriorates after they retire. As the saying goes, "the stronger the wind, the stronger the trees".

When our filtration system is clogged and broken down, the squeezers are processed in a way that creates emotions like stress, anxiety or fear. We often end up feeling like we have no control over these un-resourceful states. It is these states that rob us of our quality of life

Stress is a choice.

So is any un-resourceful state such as anxiety, fear, anger, overwhelm and frustration. The choice is made in the same way you can choose any resourceful state such as happiness, excitement, passion and motivation.

If our states are a choice, why don't we all choose the good stuff? Because stress is a behavioral pattern, they have become a habit. Most of us don't realize it's a choice. And if we do, our system is probably a little clogged or rusty from lack of use.

Notice your feelings the next time you get upset at something. Initially you may feel that the anger (or whatever your emotion is) is just happening to you, you have no control over it. This is because you are on autopilot. However there is a point where you realize you can either stay angry or you can move on. This is your moment of choice. As you take your controls off autopilot the choice happens at the beginning and not at the end.

I'm sure you have had the experience of being in a

"bad" mood as you were driving down the road when your favorite song comes on the radio. What do you do, turn it off because you don't want to feel good? If you did, that was a choice. Most likely you got caught up in the song and forgot all about your problem, at least for the 3 or 4 minutes while the song was on. Or maybe you were in a really good mood until you got back to the office to see the pile of papers that have accumulated in your in-basket. State change? You choose to focus on the stack of papers instead of whatever it was you were thinking about before you saw the stack of papers.

You are the Orange

This time, imagine you are the orange. The skin is the image we present to the world. We shine it up all pretty and out we go. For the most part it is quite thick. However, if we don't take care of it, it can get very bruised.

The flesh is our emotions. The condition of your emotions is dependent on how well we filter everything that is going on around us. If you have a healthy attitude towards life and take good care of your body; you will be filled with wonderful sweet orange juice.

On the other hand, if you blame everyone else for your problems and feel your life is out of control, you never get the good breaks; you will be filled with rotten, sour juice.

Or maybe you have given up hope. The stress and the anxiety of day to day life has worn you down. You will be all dried out inside.

It is our emotional state that determines how we respond and react to the challenges of day-to-day life. If you are the first orange, when you get squeezed, you are able to share your wonderful juice with any one you wish.

The second orange, you explode your rotten juice on everyone around you. And if you are all dried out, you have nothing to share at all.

What you have on the inside is what you have to share. After a while, if you get rotten enough or dried out enough, it will show up on the skin. Even though we may try, eventually it becomes impossible to hide what is really going on inside.

The Choice

The filter, that which determines whether what we take in is sweet or sour, is the thing that allows us to be human. The filter is the *choices* we make. The orange is at the effect of its environment. Did it grow up in a good orchard or was it raised on the wrong side of the field? Was it exposed to a toxic environment or was it raised in an organic environment filled with lots of nurturing sunshine?

We are not at the effect of the environment, our surrounding or even our upbringing. As adults, we can choose how we want to respond to our challenges, past present and future.

You can only give what you have.

This is not a new concept. Jesus taught "The Kingdom of Heaven is within." All the great masters have taught of this. If it is true, we certainly have an abundance to share. To me, newborn babies are a wonderful example of this. Have you ever noticed how incredibly blissful people are around newborns? This is because all they have on the inside is love. That is why people feel so much love towards them.

There is one more part to the orange. The most important part, the seed. It is its centre. It has the potential to bloom a thousand orchards. No matter how rotten or dried out you may get, your seed can provide you with the strength to overcome any obstacle. Your seed is your untapped potential to begin again and be the orange you always wanted to be.

But what if I am really, really rotten?

There is hope. In fact, there is a lot more than hope. We all get rotten or dried out at times. Just like we are all filled with the juice of life at times.

We will go into detail how you can take active control of your state in Chapter 5. What is important to understand right now, is that what goes in comes out.

"*Let no one ever come to you without leaving better and happier.*"
Mother Teresa

Chapter 2 THE FORMULA FOR SUCCESS

The first question we need to answer is what is success? Everyone has a different definition of success. For the purposes of this book, I will be defining success as having a Constantly Increasing Quality of Life regardless of money or position.

Success is not determined by external factors. The new job title or the money in the bank account can disappear faster than it took to create them… much faster. Relationships, possessions, money all come and go. The only thing that remains constant is who we are on the inside. The added bonus is that when we are generating states like happiness, security and love from the inside-out, it allows us the freedom to enjoy the material success that much more.

Now, I am not suggesting that you move to the top of a mountain and spend the rest of your life meditating. The greatest fulfillment in life comes from being of value to other people. It is for this reason the success formula is so powerful.

Personal Growth X Service = Success

The more you grow, the more you can adapt to and eventually thrive on change. The more you thrive on change, the more you can focus on being of value to others. The more value (service) you can give to others the more abundance you will receive.

In other words,
the more you grow, the more you can give,
the more you will receive.

How do you grow? Read, listen to tapes, take courses, watch PBS. Be an active participant in life, not a spectator. We can learn the three most important factors in growing by watching young children. First of all they are curious about everything. They never stop asking why and how and trying to understand even the smallest things. Secondly they take action. They get actively involved in the learning process. They don't sit back and say, "prove it to me." When they learn something they immediately go out and try it. They keep doing it until they have it. And last but not least, they have fun. They wake up each day with a true joy for living. This is how you grow. The happiest people are the people that can retain these child like qualities as they mature into responsible adults.

The Value to the Organization

Most organizations are beginning to realize the importance of well-rounded employees. The happier and better adjusted they are in their personal lives, the better able they are to bring that excitement to the job.

However, it is not the responsibility of any organization to make you grow. They certainly need to provide the opportunities for growth, but it is you that must make the decision to be a student of life.

The 3 Levels of Growth

From the moment we are conceived, our life is a journey of growth. Physically, mentally and spiritually we grow and develop. There are three ways in which we can grow in this lifetime. Which one we choose is entirely up to us and will determine the quality of life we will experience. Imagine each of these 3 levels is like a muscle. The more it is used the bigger it gets. Since no one sets out to fail, we will often do what has worked in the past, even if it is not the most effective approach.

Reactive Growth *(also known as the school of hard knocks)*

Life will keep giving us lessons until we learn them. The way life teaches these lessons is through challenges. All challenges, ranging from that annoying little sound your spouse makes to a life threatening illness. In order to survive these challenges, we must grow. We then become stronger and better able to handle the next challenge. **Reactive growth means that we wait for the challenge to occur and then hope we have the strength to overcome it.** These people build their muscles through crisis management, jumping from one fire to the next and thinking they are getting a terrific workout.

The problem with this type of growth is that it can be very stressful and emotionally draining. We can get so caught up in the drama of what is happening that we may miss the lesson we need to learn. The emotional stress of handling the challenge can help to create new challenges and the next thing we know is that we are living life going from one crisis to another. Years can go by and we are still working on the same lessons, often very stressed and extremely bitter.

This is the slowest form of growth because it can often take years, even a lifetime to learn a single lesson. At this level, life is seen as a struggle, something to be survived.

Pre-emptive Growth.

Anticipating the challenges and the opportunities (actually these are the same thing aren't they?), that life has to offer, some people choose to go out in advance and learn what they need to be prepared to handle whatever life hands them.

This includes things like university and college to meet the demands of an increasingly demanding marketplace. This type of growth tends to focus on the marketplace skills. They develop intellectually. The belief that a good job is paramount to a quality of life is common at this level of growth.

The challenge with this approach is that even though the individual may have the skill set to thrive, they may be so emotionally drained by the stress and pace of life that they cannot access their potential. Even though the university degree or past accomplishments will help to create a sense of certainty, it may still be a very frustrating path because core issues such as security, fear of failure or self worth will keep reoccurring.

Accelerated Growth

This is how people who are hungry for life approach it. They take full responsibility for their own growth and dive deep into the experience of life. They get in touch with who they are and they understand that a life worth living is a life given in service. They gain an understanding of their specific purpose and move their life in the direction of that purpose.

They develop themselves emotionally, physically, spiritually as well as intellectually. They take care of their health. Sleep, eat and exercise in a way that will support them. They read books and attend workshops to develop emotional strength to be able to handle the unpredictability of life. They will use tools like mediation to help wipe away the effects of stress get in touch with who they really are. Much more often than not they will have a deep spiritual connection. Whether it is through a religious practice are more of a free flowing approach, they are connected to the abundant creativity of the universe.

People on the path of accelerated growth have a goal of freedom. The freedom to experience life at it fullest. The freedom to give the very best of themselves, everyday to everyone and in everything they do.

This is where the greatest joy in life is found. Yes there is still pain, but the pain is seen for what it really is, the opportunity to grow, expand and experience life at a new level.

It is at this level that we can truly be of Service.
It is at this level that we realize that every
moment is a moment of truth.

Personal Leadership

Success comes to those who can focus their energy and talents to produce outstanding results in their given field. Quality of life comes to those who can extend that focus to all areas of their life. That skill is called Personal Leadership.

Personal Leadership is the ability to create a constantly increasing quality of life regardless of external circumstances. To be the writer, producer, director and star of your life and to conduct yourself in such a manner that allows all those around you to be the same for their lives.

Personal Leadership is the fundamental skill that is required to be of service to others. It is extremely difficult to be of service to others if you are unable to take control of your own life. This doesn't mean you have to be Ted Turner or Bill Gates before you can wow your customers. It does mean that you need to have the ability to rise above the challenges of day to day life so that you can tap into your potential.

The 4 Keys of Personal Leadership

1. ***Energy.***
   Every goal, dream and desire you have will require energy to create it. Momentum begins and ends with your energy level. Energy is created through passion. Passion for what you do and whom you serve. You must engage your heart to tap into your passion.

   Have you ever noticed how much energy you have when you are doing something you love? Working on a hobby or playing with your children time flies by and you could go forever. You have engaged your heart and tapped into your passion.

   Once your passion is engaged, your health must sustain your energy. It's the way you eat, drink, sleep and move. More of the good things and less of the bad.

2. ***Personal Responsibility.***
   The ability – to – respond. In any moment, in any circumstance in life, regardless of what is going on, we have the ability to choose our response. This does not mean it's "our fault". It simply means, "here we are, how do we make the best of it." It also means that when it is your fault you step-up and make it right. The individual who truly understands the power of personal responsibility understands there is no fault, no blame, just the opportunity for growth.

3. ***Be Proactive***
   An outstanding quality of life comes to those who decide to create the life of their dreams instead of dreaming about a life. Wowing the customer does not happen by waiting and reacting to the challenges. It happens by anticipating needs and preempting obstacles.

4. ***Always Growing and Learning.***
   In life we are always growing and expanding or we are shrinking and dieing. The choice is yours.

"The price of Greatness is responsibility."
Winston Churchill

Chapter 3
3 LEVELS OF COMMUNICATION

Success in any area of life comes down to your ability to communicate. If you are in sales, obviously you need to have the ability to effectively communicate to the customer how your product or service meets their needs. (That's assuming you were communicating effectively enough to discover their needs in the first place).
In your relationship, communication is the foundation that allows you and your partner to freely express your needs and connect with each other. If the communication breaks down, the relationship breaks down.

Effective external communication is a key to success in any environment. Being able to communicate so your children will listen, or asking your boss for that raise or getting the team to "buy in". Of course, it is critical to outstanding service. However, external communication, or as we will refer to it, 1 on 1 communication is only *one* of the three levels you must master to experience success.

1. ***Internal Communication:*** Our internal communication is the way we manage our state. The better you communicate with yourself, the better you can manage how you feel. Quality of life is determined by your ability, or lack thereof, too communicate with yourself.

The value of internal communication breaks down like this, *the better your state, the better your actions. The better your actions, the better your results. The better your results, the better your rewards.*

2. ***1 on 1 Communication:*** The best way you can be of value to other people is to know what they want, and then help them to get it. One of the most valued skills in the market place is the ability to put someone else in a better state, because everyone wants to feel good.

   Every time two people have an interaction, energy is exchanged. You walk away feeling better than before the interaction, or worse.

   The importance of 1 on 1 communication breaks down like this: *the better you communicate with someone else, the better you under stand their needs and the better they understand what you have to offer.*

3. ***Team Communication:*** championship teams seem to communicate almost telepathically. One player passes the ball to a given spot and magically a teammate shows up just in time to make the play. Or when you pick up the phone to ask for a new set of data and your assistant walks in your office with the information.

Outstanding teamwork comes when each individual team member takes personal responsibility for being the best they possibly can at their role on the team. Teams are not just limited to our work. We are on teams in our families, communities, where there are two or more people working towards a common objective.

In the end, the value of being an outstanding team player is in the synergy. Synergy is when 2+2=5. This is the value of teamwork.

"The Quality of your life is the Quality of your Communication"
Anthony Robbins

Chapter 4
YOUR STARRING ROLE

Congratulations. You have just landed the lead role in an up coming movie. The critics are very excited about this one. The buzz is it has the potential to be a huge block-buster success. The challenge is that there is only an outline for a script and most of the scenes will be impromptu. To top it all off, it is going to be filmed in live action. No re-takes or doing the scene over fifty times to get it right. You have one shot at each scene. This is of course a huge risk so it could also turn out to be a massive direct to video flop.

The reason there is so much buzz around this movie is because of the star, *you*. They feel that you have the talent and the skills to win an Academy Award for Best Actor/Actress. They are saying this is the role you were born to play.

The quality of your performance will be determined by the amount of effort you put into the role. You already have everything you need for it on the INSIDE.

Because you are so suited for this movie, you have also been given the role of director as well. This is by far the most important role in the movie. Even though it will be live action, you will be using many different cameras to capture all of the action. It is your job to determine what angle is the best one to use to make it the best scene possible.

Are you excited? You should be, because it's for real. The role is your life. The scenes of the movie are your day-to-day experiences. You literally have direct control of the quality of this movie. Being in the lead role, you determine how much you put in to each scene. Are you just coasting along trying to get through the scene without incident or are you putting your heart and soul into to make it the blockbuster it has the potential to be.

You see most people do not realize they are in the lead role of their own lives. Or if they do, they feel it is being directed by their obligations, their boss or even a higher power. This is simply not true. When you were born, you were given the rights to this production of your life. Even though your early years may not have been the movie you hoped for, as an adult, you have complete control over this production.

Does this mean that you can control all of the events and people around you? Certainly not. What it does mean is that you are in control of how you respond to these outside events and what camera angles you choose to ***show on the screen of your mind.*** It is not the events that make this movie a success. Some of you will have a fairly smooth ride, and some of you will have to overcome challenges that will test you at the deepest level. The level of success will be determined by the amount of control you take over your role.

Your quality of life is not determined by your challenges or circumstances, it is determined by how you choose to respond to them.

The more control you take over this production, the better the movie will be. You can have all of the adventure, comedy, action and romance that you want. It is all right here. You don't need a bigger budget or a better-looking co-star. There is no special effects that have to be added or sets changed.

Have you ever gone to a movie that you enjoyed so much that you were telling all of your friends they just had to go? Is your life a movie people just have to go and see or is it the one everyone avoids?

"I slept and dreamt that life was joy.
I awoke and found that life was service.
I acted and, behold, service was joy."

Rabindranath Tagore

The 4 Laws of Service

Chapter 5
LAW #1
BE IN A RESOURCEFUL STATE
YOU CAN ONLY GIVE WHAT YOU HAVE

This is the first law of Outstanding Service. The quality of your movie will be determined by how much ***you*** are enjoying it. In other words, the better the state you are in, obviously the more you are enjoying your movie. If you are enjoying the movie of your life you have that enjoyment on the INSIDE to share with the people you come in contact with during your scenes.

As we have talked about in the opening chapter, Service Happens in a Moment. Wowing the customer is created when the person delivering the service is in a great state and therefore shares their excitement, enthusiasm or congruency, whatever it is they genuinely feel about their product or service, with the customer.

What is a resourceful state? It is a feeling of flexibility and focus that will allow you to handle whatever obstacle may come up. Some people call it the zone. You know the place, no matter what is happening you have the confidence, creativity and sense of humor to handle it. Your energy seems endless and time goes by in a flash. This is the ideal state for providing outstanding service.

As a parent, this is where you can really enjoy being

with your children and be the nurturing example they will need to grow up with a high level of self-esteem. In a relationship, this is the place where you are able to keep the spark alive for decades. This is the state that allows you to have the energy to go out and make a difference on the issues that matter to you the most.

It is by taking control of your own state that you are able to create a Constantly Increasing Quality of Life.

A resourceful state is any state that allows you to access increased levels of your potential. The better your state, the better your actions, the better your actions the better your results. The better your results the better your quality of life.

Exercise: Make a list of at least 3 resourceful states you want to experience for each of your roles in life.
Eg. Career - Creativity, Certainty, intelligence etc
Parent - Playful, loving, resourceful etc
Spouse - Nurturing, listening etc

Step #1
State is a Choice

As the producer of your movie, the first thing you have to do is make the decision to take over the production.

Most people in our world today have given the rights to their movie over to their parents by constantly blaming them for a poor upbringing or to the spouse that left them for someone else. They turn it over to the media that reinforces their deepest fears about their weight or attractiveness. They have bought into the myth that you can buy happiness, love or health. We have been conditioned all of our lives that we are not in control.

If you were the customer, who would you rather do business with, the person who is directing and starring in a Academy Award winning blockbuster, or someone who's movie went straight to the B movie section at the video store?

How do you make the choice? Make the decision. In order to take control you can no longer blame others, for anything. You must take responsibility for ***you*** in every situation. This does not mean you don't hold people accountable for their actions. It means you don't blame them for "making me so mad" or "if only you would...". They don't "make you mad". It is your response that makes you mad.

The only way to experience true freedom in this lifetime is to choose your own state.

Exercise: Make a list of the states you want to experience less. i.e. stress, anger, fatigue, overwhelm
Make a list of the states you want to experience more. i.e. confidence, happiness, creativity, passion

Step #2
Direct Your Focus

The first way to change your state is to change what you are focusing on.

Imagine that you are the director for a televised broadcast of a football game. You are sitting in the big control truck outside of the stadium. On the wall in front of you are a number of monitors. For this example let's say there are 6. On each of these monitors is a different camera angle. On camera 1 is the quarterback. #2 is the most likely receiver. #3 is the running back. #4 is the defensive line. # 5 is the linebacker and #6 is the head cheerleader.

As the play unfolds, our perception of the game is determined by what camera angle we see. We will also make assumptions about the game by what angle we see. If the director chooses to show use the offensive lineman grabbing the facemask of his blocking assignment, we may determine that it is a rough and dirty game. If we see the quarterback throwing a long touchdown pass to a wide-open receiver, we may assume that the other teams defense is having a bad game. If the camera shot is of an angry coach on the sidelines, we might assume that he is upset with how his team is playing. Or he may choose to show us a close-up of a group of fans for team A who are cheering their faces off, and we may assume that team A is having a great game.

Some of these assumptions we made may be true, others not. You may not have made these assumptions on the first time a given scene was shown. However you may form that opinion if you are shown similar scenes over and over. Let's take the screaming fans as an example. Perhaps they get shown 3 or 4 times. The director likes this particular group because they are so lively. What this camera angle does not show is that they are the only fans for team A in a stadium of 70,000 people and they would be cheering regardless because they have taken several trips to the beer counter.

Perhaps the coach is thrilled with his team's play and he is upset at one of his coaches upstairs for calling a bad play. The point is that in any given situation there are many different camera angels available, and whatever one is chosen will often determine our perception (the state we choose to feel) about that situation.

How your Mind works

Your mind is very much like the control booth in the production truck. Your senses are the cameras, picking up an almost limitless amount of information. Your brain then decides what information to show on the screen of your mind. For some people the movie is played out in pictures, for others it is just words and for some it is feelings. Most of us have a combination of all three. It is these movies that effect how we feel.

The Control Booth

There is a switch in the control booth that allows you to decide what screen you are going to view. That switch is called ***questions.***

You can control your focus by the questions you ask yourself. Simply put, ask yourself a great question, you will have a great focus therefore a great state. Ask yourself a bad question you will have a bad focus, therefore a bad state.

The Car Wreck

It was a horribly cold January day. I was on the 3-hour drive from my home in Calgary to a workshop in Edmonton. The road conditions were poor so I was driving 90 km/hr, 20 below the speed limit. At the last minute I had decided to take my father in laws Ford Explorer. He and my mother in law were out of the country for 6 weeks so they left the truck with us in case we needed it. I thought it would help with the road conditions.

The ride was going well. I was listening to a book tape and enjoying the time to mentally prepare for the workshop with a group of newly appointed senior managers. Suddenly the back of the truck slid out to the side. Before I could do anything the truck was into a full spin. It spun around three or four times in the middle of the highway before it hit the ditch. Because of all the snow piled up on the side of the road the truck immediately rolled over. It slid about 50 yards on its roof.

When it finally stopped I was pinned to the roof by the drivers seat. Fortunately, I did not have my seat belt on because the roof had collapsed to only about 3 inches above the steering wheel. My very first thought was that of gratefulness my children were not in the vehicle.

The second thought was "this is great, I get to buy Sham a new truck!" In that moment that was the focus I chose. After I had walked away from the wreck without even so much as a bruise, I realized what 2 incredible gifts I had been given. First, that I was alive. Very cool.

The second was more subtle but no less profound, I truly control how I feel, regardless of external challenges. I was able to "react" in such a "positive" way because I had conditioned my self over years of always asking, "what's great about this" any time I ran up against a challenge. And though it was a valuable tool from the first time I asked it, here I was in a life or death moment of truth and my natural un-efforted reaction was, "great I get to buy Sham a new truck". Oh, and by the way, the insurance money did get him a better truck than he had before.

Positive Thinking?

Positive thinking has got a bad rap in recent years. Mostly because many of the people who extol it's virtues are using it incorrectly. As the company is sliding into bankruptcy, they walk around the office asking everyone if they are having a great day. This doesn't help anyone.

What we want to create is solution thinking. By asking questions we can direct the most powerful computer on the planet (your mind) to not just feel great, but also find the solution and take the required action.

Anatomy of a State

When people are faced with a challenge there are three main states they tend to experience. Here are the three states and the focus that creates them.

Fear - Why is this happening to me?
- Why am I so (stupid, lazy etc)...

These questions do not lead to a solution. All they do is send you on a downward spiral of frustration, stress and perhaps even depression.

Hope - Everything is going to be okay.
- How many lottery tickets should I buy?

Hoping that someone or something else is going to rescue us is a sure way to get stuck at this place in our lives, for the rest of our lives. Hoping more often than not results in inaction.

Certainty - What's great about this?
- What would happen if...?
- What can I learn from this?

How and what questions help to gain clarity and then focus that clarity into action.

Creating a Solution Focus

A. Begin with How or what. Avoid the endless loop of why questions.

B. Make sure it puts you in a resourceful state.
I.e. what's great about this?

C. Make it as specific as possible. Ask for exactly what you want. Focus on what you want, not what you don't want.
I.e. I want more money. - How can I generate $50,000 by August 15th and enjoy the process?

D. Ask the question with the intention of getting an answer. Just like when you are having a conversation, if you ask a question and want an answer to it, you have wait for the person to respond. The same is true of your mind.

E. Ask as many times with many different questions to get the solution you need.

Making it a Habit

Exercise 1. *Monitor your habitual questions and self talk over a week. Carry around a note book* *and record them in the book. At the end of the week make a list of all the words, phrases and questions that do not support you.*

2. *Begin to eliminate these words, phrases and questions from your habitual vocabulary.*

3. *Make at list of at least 5 new question using the Solution Question Formula. Write these questions on a 3x5 index card and place them in places were you will see them often.*

4. *Begin asking your self these questions as often as possible for at least three weeks so you can begin to develop the habit of solution thinking.*

How bad is it really?

Your state acts like a magnifying glass. It takes whatever is going on around you and magnifies it as if it is showing it to you on the viewing screen in your mind. Your state also acts like a magnet, attracting to it similar states.

Positive attracts Positive
Negative attracts negative

Step #3
The Better You Move
The Better You Feel

Your mind and your body are intimately connected. The mind/body connection has gained tremendous popularity over the past decade with the work of people like Deepak Chopra and Andrew Weil. However, as these men acknowledge, they are simply bringing forward the knowledge the sages of eastern spirituality have practiced for centuries. What you feel in your mind you feel in your body, what you feel in your body you feel in your mind.

Have you ever noticed how great you feel after a workout? This is because your body loves to move. You have triggered off powerful hormones that naturally make you feel great.

Every State has a Physiology

Every state has a corresponding physiology. This physiology can either help *create* the state by signals it sends to your brain, or is created by the signals it receives from your brain.

When you are stressed your body will move in a certain way. When you are fearful it will move another way. The changes may be subtle, but powerful. If I asked you to describe a depressed person could you do it? Of course. Head down shoulders slouched, listless and shallow breathing. How about a confident person? Shoulders back, head up and eyes focused. Breathing is deep and steady.

Creating a State with Physiology

1. ***Awareness:*** Start to become aware of how powerfully your physiology effects your state. Take notes. When you feel great write down how you are using your body. When you are stressed, do the same thing. With any state, notice how changing your body changes that initial state.

The next time you are feeling an unwanted emotion like stress, take a big breath, sit up straight and put a big smile on your face.

> *Just as a professional athlete understands the importance of their mental game to being outstanding, you need to understand the importance of your physiology to creating the quality of life you desire.*

2. ***Breath.*** Breath is essential to life. You can only last a few minutes without. In eastern traditions, how you use your breath is considered to be one of the key practices on a path to enlightenment. In yoga, your breath is considered as important as the movement itself.

   Notice your breath when you are stressed. Typically it will be very shallow, you may even find you are holding it at times. It is next to impossible to create a resourceful state when there is no oxygen getting into your body.

   Practice taking deep breathes. All day long, especially if you want to change your state. Put an index card on your desk and write BREATH. A great breath to practice is a basic yoga breath. Breathe in, down to your diaphragm for a count of 1, hold for a count of 4 and exhale for a count of 2.

   Try one, breathe in to the count of 4, hold to 16 and exhale to 8. Now do that 10 times 3 times a day. This breathing pattern will help to relax and energize you. Enjoy!

3. ***Movement.*** It has been said that Motion creates

Emotion. A powerful confident physiology can help to create a powerful confident state. When you move your body, that movement sends a signal to your brain. If it is an excited movement, smile on your face and bright eyed, your brain is told to be excited. If it is a stressful movement, like tensing the shoulders, clenching the jaw and wringing your hands, your brain gets the signal to be stressed.

If you want to create better states, the quickest way to create them is to move your body differently. You can't expect a different result if you keep the same strategy.

4. ***Model.*** Take your list of resourceful states from step #1 and create them with your physiology. Pretend you are an actor and for your role you have to be confident. Really create it in your body. Now, write it down so you will remember it and then practice. The more you practice the easier it will be for your body to return to this state. Eventually your body/mind will naturally be in the states you train yourself to be in.

Step #4
What can be measured can be improved

The only way to improve something is to measure it, notice the results you are getting and then develop a plan for improvement. The same is true with your state. It is something that can be measured, and therefore can be improved upon like any other skill.

The best way to measure it is to compare your state level to a scale. For this example lets use your level of energy as the state we are going to measure.

0 1 2 3 4 5 6 7 8 9 10

On this scale, 0 represents no energy at all. Bored, tired and listless. You know, the way you often feel on Wednesday afternoon during an extremely busy week. The 10 represents being completely full of life. Energized and vital. The way you feel when you return from holidays.

On this scale, determine what number you are at. Where is you level of energy? Circle it or write it down on a piece of paper. Now the objective is to improve your state (increase your level of energy) using the tools from Step 2 and 3 and change focus and physiology.

So, let's say you are at a level 4. The first step is to move to a level 5. So sit up in your chair, take a deep breath and look up. Did this create more energy? It should have. Maybe not a lot, but at least a little bit. Now think about; focus on something that you are really looking forward to doing this week. If you don't have anything, make it up! Are you now at a 6? This is how you can measure and then improve your state. Now to put it over the edge, go and put on your favorite CD and crank it up. Jump around like you just won a million dollars.

What's your state like now? You should have increased your level of energy quite a bit. Now this is just a quick example, but this is the same idea you will use to improve your state over the long term.

Obviously, outstanding service comes from being in a level 10 state. This scale is used in the same way to measure all of the states you have to choose from, not just energy. You can measure excitement, creativity, confidence, love, passion, gratefulness, and any state you want to experience.

The idea is to check in throughout the day and determine your level of state. Of course the first things you need to do is to decide what is the best state for you to be in right now. Once you have decided on the most resourceful state, measure it on the 0-10 scale. If the ideal level is 8-10, then we need to move from where we are to there.

You have already learned the power of focus and physiology. So move your body and change your focus.

Two excellent questions to improve your state in this situation are

1. What has to happen for me to be in a level __ state right now?
2. How can I create a level___ right now and enjoy the process?

Taking control of your state is the most critical step to creating a Constantly Increasing Quality of Life

"If you don't take control of your body, it will become your master instead of your servant."
Stephen Covey

Chapter 6
LAW #2
STAY IN A RESOURCEFUL STATE

Creating a resourceful state is a very valuable tool. It will dramatically impact the quality of your life and your ability to deliver outstanding service. However, it is really not that valuable when it's all gone by 9 am. The real value of state comes in when it gets tested. Anyone can be in a good mood when all is well.

The idea is that this resourceful state is not a face you put on, instead it is a ***self- perpetuating state,*** one that does not come from the level of personality, but instead is created from the level of who you really are, an infinite being. It is in this place a resourceful state can easily be maintained, because it is your natural state.

Stress and frustration often come from trying to be someone you're not. At our core (inside) we are all joyous, blissful beings with unlimited potential. A beautiful invaluable diamond. Somewhere along the way we buried this treasure deep inside and covered it with layers of personality to protect it from the world. In order to be truly happy and live a life of purposeful service we must bring the diamond to the surface and allow its value to be experienced by everyone we touch.

It is only when we bring the most valuable treasure of all to the surface, who we really are, that we are able to effortlessly exist in a resourceful state.

Step #1
Present Moment Awareness

Worry is the great thief of life. There are so many people in our culture who spend countless amounts of energy and significant portions of their day worrying about events and possible outcomes that they have absolutely no control over. And worse yet, the vast majority of these "events" never even occur.

Equally as destructive is the amount of time some people spend rehashing old events from the past, reliving the pain over and over again (more about this in step two).

In order to maximize our potential it is essential that we learn from the past, prepare for the future and live in the present moment.

There are 6 steps to overcoming worry. Think about something that is worrying you and grab out a piece of paper and answer the questions.

1. ***Identify the Challenge***. Often our emotions get in the way and we can lose site of what the real challenge is. Clarify it in one or two sentences. Make it a specific as possible.
   i.e. *The company is restructuring and my future is uncertain.*

2. ***What are all of the possible outcomes and what***

that means? For some problems there can almost be an endless list of possibilities, so list the two or three key scenarios.

i.e. ***A***. *I will lose my job - I may not be able to find another right away. We could use up all of our savings, go broke.*

B. *I will have to learn new skills - If I can't do the new job well, I may get fired.*

This stage help will you to get clear on what you are really worried about. In this case, we are really worried about losing our job and experiencing financial ruin.

3. ***Worst Scenario.*** Make a simple statement that outlines what is the worst possible outcome.

    i.e. *We will be financially ruined. I won't be able to take care of my family.*

4. ***Develop an Action Plan.*** Take your worst case scenarios and develop a plan. What will you do? How will you do it? When, with who, etc.

    i.e. *Get our finances in order so we know our options. Finish my small business plan. Set up a meeting with George to see if I can find out what skills I will need if they transfer my position.*

5. ***What I am actually in control of?*** Of all the things that are affecting this challenge, what do you actually control? Make the list. What you will discover is that the main thing you have any control over is how you are going to respond to this obstacle.

i.e. *I am in control of my state.*
I am in control of how we decide to spend the money we currently have.

6. ***What are at least three things that are great about this challenge?*** You already understand the power of focus. This is a great way to build momentum for your action steps.
   i.e. *I can start the small business I always wanted to. If they give me a new position, I get to develop a new skill set. Regardless of what happens, we are going to get our finances in order, something we should have done year ago.*

7. ***What can I do right now, today?***
   Make a list and start with number 1, right now.

Instead of worrying, you can now put your energy into your action plan. If the worst case scenario happens, you're prepared. If it doesn't, you're ahead of the game.

Step #2
Choose the Meaning

Events happen. The computer crashes. The wrong order gets sent out. Your stock portfolio drops off the chart. Your son decides to write off your brand new car. No matter how hard we try, events like these, and worse, are going to happen in our lives. The bus just keeps on rolling and we can either get thrown off with each bump or we can ride them out and get to our destination intact.

Creating an outstanding state over the long term is based on your ability to decide what each "set back" is going to mean. That's right, you get to decide what these events are going to mean to you in your life. *Nothing in life has any meaning other than the meaning that you give it.*

Look back at your own life. Remember one of the most difficult times you ever experienced. At the time, it was probably a very intense, maybe even devastating experience. As the years have passed and you are able to look back more objectively, you have probably seen the value of the lesson you learned from that experience. It is usually the most trying experiences of our life that later become the most valuable. So why wait 10 or 15 years to decide it was valuable, decide right now?

Take an obstacle you are experiencing in your life right now. If you were to attach a positive meaning to it, what would it be? If you can't think of one, make one up.

To your mind, reality is whatever you tell it is. Your reality is created by how you communicate to yourself. The better your communication the better your reality.

Step #3
Be Self-Referral

Abraham Maslow, the great philosopher, said that one of the keys to being a self-actualized person was to become "independent of the *good* opinion of other people". This is much easier said than done.

As children, most of us were taught not to worry about what the others kids thought of us. Not to go along with the crowd, be our own person. Yet, in the next breath, we were told to get a haircut and improve our grades because "what will the neighbors think?". Many of us received this contradiction throughout our childhood. On the one hand, we were told not to care what others thought of us. On the other hand we saw most of the "grown-ups" around us spending huge amounts of time, energy and money to keep up with the Jones's.

The great North American dream is all about "how do I stack up?" How do I compare to everyone else? People decide their own personal value based on how they compare to the family, friends and co-workers around them. Even worse, they compare themselves to the people they see on TV and in magazines. There is nothing wrong with using television and the media for entertainment, but remember it is just that, entertainment, not a template for how to live your life.

Becoming self-referral is so critical to creating a self perpetuating state because when we are no longer attached to the opinion others have of us, they can no longer bring us "down" by a simple comment or how they react to us.

When we are attached to what others think of us, we give away our freedom.

So, how do I do it?

1. ***Value who you are***. In all of the universe, there is no one exactly like you. Cherish that uniqueness.

2. ***Be silent***. The best way to get in touch with the greater part of yourself is through silence. Meditation is an excellent tool. Another wonderful idea is to just be silent for a period of time each week. That means for an hour or two with no talking, television or even reading. Just allow your mind to quiet. At first you will be filled

with self-talk as your mind tries to figure out what's going on. However as you show your ego that you are in control, not it, your mind will quiet down.

3. ***Non-Judgment.*** Stop judging yourself. Stop judging others. It is difficult to value who you are when you are busy judging others for being who they are.

Step #4
Get & Stay Healthy

Your health is probably the most valuable asset you have. If you have had trouble with yours, you already realize this. There is nothing more draining than being ill. Even the little things like headaches, stiff back and the common cold can throw your state out the window.

Take care of your self. If you don't, no one else will.

1. ***Eat right.*** Most people eat a dead diet. Dead meat, over cooked vegetable and packaged foods. Eat lots of fresh fruits and vegetables, every day. Juicing is an excellent way to get the vitamins, minerals and enzymes your body requires for optimum health.

2. ***Drink.*** Your body is 70% water so it requires large amounts of water. Sorry, coffee and cola do not count but fresh juice and herbal teas do.

3. ***Exercise***. Your body was designed to be in motion. There probably isn't a lot of motion going

on behind your desk. So get up and get moving. Even going for a walk on a regular basis can go a long way to improving your over all health.

4. ***Rest***. Your body needs rest. There is a natural cycle that your body wants to follow. Early to bed, early to rise isn't just a corny saying. Most of us do the late to bed, early to rise approach and then have to fill up on caffeine and stress to get us through the day.

Some scientists are now saying we have the potential to live to be 120 years old. What an amazing gift. However, it isn't going to be that much fun if your body gives out 20-30 years early. Your body is your temple, your vehicle for fulfilling your purpose here on earth. Treat it with the care and respect it deserves.

Step #5
Surround Yourself with People who Support you

Build a team that will support you. No one individual can win the championship on their own. Even in individual sports, they have a team of coaches, trainers and supporters. You need to have people around you who build you up, not tear you down. All too often people will try to be like a burning torch. They burn intensely and brightly for a short time, and then when they burn out, that's it. But if you are a log on a bonfire, if you burn out you will have your friends to light you back up.

One of the most difficult decisions people often face

is leaving their past behind so they can create a brighter future. However, this is a critical step because you cannot grow if other peoples fears and negativity keep chewing away at your roots.

This doesn't mean you surround your self with a group of "yes-men" or "groupies". Support means they can be honest with you and share the same or similar vision for the future. You can tell if it is a healthy supportive relationship if there is a consistent exchange of value.

The action plan:

1. ***Eliminate the Negative:*** Distance yourself from the water cooler crowd. Some people choose to complain and gossip about challenges instead of creating solutions. What a great way to destroy your quality of life.

2. ***Surround with Supportive:*** Who are the people on the fast track in your company? Who are the parents in your community who have great family relationships? Find these people and become involved in the same professional groups or community associations. Remember that people who are producing results also want to surround themselves with people who are making things happen.

Maintaining a resourceful state regardless of what is going on around you takes practice. However once mastered, it will be one of the most valuable skills you will ever develop in your life. It is not what we do once in a while that creates a constantly increasing quality of life, it is what we do consistently, day in day out.

"The Wizard knows that to be truly alive ,
she must die to the past in every moment.
To be alive now is to be dead to the past.
To be alive know is to have
life-centred awareness,
present moment awareness."
Return of Merlin, Deepak Chopra

The 4 Laws of Service

Chapter 7
LAW #3
PUT THE CUSTOMER IN AN OUTSTANDING STATE

The better the state of the customer, the better they are going to receive whatever service you provide. As we have already talked about, your state acts like a filter. If you are in a good state, you tend to filter things in a positive manner. If you are in a bad state, you tend to filter things in a negative way.

We have all had the experience of dealing with the customer that no matter what we do, they are not happy. This is because they are in a stuck state. That does not mean they do not have a legitimate concern. What it means is **they are filtering whatever we do, provide, or offer from a negative perspective**. I'm sure you have had the experience yourself, when you were the dissatisfied customer, of deciding that no matter what they do, you weren't going to be satisfied. From this place there is very little we can do to make things right.

The key is to help the customer into a receptive state. I had to learn this lesson the hard way. On this occasion the customer was my wife. She is also my business partner and the amazing mother of our wonderful children. I was getting frustrated by the lack of, or poor response I was getting to some ideas I was sharing with her. I would be in my office home, have a lightening bolt of an idea, and run upstairs to share it with her. I put myself in state. I stayed in state; still I was not getting my outcome.

She tried very hard. She would listen and give input, yet I could tell the ideas were not having the impact I thought they should. Why? Lipi was in the wrong state. She was in mommy mode. Her mind was on house cleaning, diapers or what's for dinner. In this instance, the key to success was to wait until she was in the office or the children had gone to bed. Had I not recognized her state was my responsibility, not hers in this context, we never would have had the valuable discussions we needed to.

Step #1
Do unto Others as you would have done to you

Occasionally, I like to play a little game when I go shopping. It's called "How will the clerk react to the American Express Platinum Card" game. I remember being at a high-end clothing store in La Jolla, California with Lipi and our brand new baby girl, Kennedy. We were having a relaxing afternoon in this beautiful seaside town, and dressed accordingly. Lipi and I tend to be mistaken for being younger than we are, especially under these conditions. We enter the store to do some shopping. We were completely ignored. In fact, you could tell the sales staff was not too thrilled to have a newborn in the store. I guess it cramped their style.

After we had made our selections we went up to the cashier. We were still getting the ice treatment when I threw down the Platinum. Well, do you want to talk about a state change? It was one of the funniest things I had ever seen. All of a sudden we were like royalty. The sales person was literally falling all over herself to serve us. She was smiling and making conversation, she even talked to Kennedy. Next thing you know there was another girl helping to bag our purchases, we were even offered a frequent shopper's card.

That is not service, that is insulting. A person's economic status, position or type of credit card should have nothing to with whether they receive good service.
The golden rule is the best rule when it comes to service. Treat every customer like they are your best customer, and they will let people know about your wonderful service.

Step #2
Direct Their Movie

Just as your state is determined by what you choose to focus on, your customer's state is determined by what they focus on. You are the one with the script in this scene, use it.

Because you are in a resourceful state, you are flexible enough to adapt to the state they are in. Whoever is more committed to their level of state, is the person who will have the greatest effect on the other person's state.

Create the scene

With each interaction you have with the customer, you should have a clear idea of how you want the interaction to turn out. By knowing your outcome you can take control of the "scene" and direct your customers focus in the direction of that outcome.

The best way to direct their focus is through asking great questions. All outstanding influencers understand the power of asking great questions. Questions give you an understanding of what the customer wants and more importantly needs. It is the way to take them from focusing on the challenge to focusing on a solution.

Develop Your Questions

Create a list of questions that can be used in various situations. It is best to create the questions ahead of time so you can focus your energy on the situation, not on thinking up questions.

Ask questions that will direct their focus in a specific direction. The most common question is "how are you today?" The challenge with this question is that almost no one waits to hear the answer, and what if the person is having a lousy day? You just reminded them. Lucky you.

Be creative. Be unique.

- What's the best thing that happened to you today?
- What was the best part of your weekend?
- What did you enjoy about…?

Now, will they answer the question, perhaps not? However, just by asking the question their mind will begin to focus on the answer. They will start searching the files of their mind and, they will be in a better state.

What would happen if…

Asking your customer "What would happen if…" and providing a possible solution opens up possibilities. It allows the person's mind to momentarily focus on what is possible and get unstuck.

Step #3
Build Rapport

There should be no surprise here. Rapport is the ability to connect with another human being at a deep level. To go beyond the "how are you today?" to a level of trust and understanding. To enter their world.

There are many powerful and sophisticated techniques for developing rapport. Once mastered they can be an invaluable tool for connecting with even the most difficult people. The challenge is, many people become so focused on the techniques that they lose sight of the person they want to connect with.

The best way to create rapport with someone is described in Dale Carnegie's classic book How to Win Friends and Influence People. Show a genuine interest in the other person. People love to connect with others who are genuinely interested in them. The key word here is genuinely.

When you sincerely try to connect with someone and enter his or her world, it is almost assured you will develop rapport with that person. The best way to do that is to ask questions and then listen intently.

Step #4
Check Your Ego at The Door

Simply put, **you need to be more concerned with helping your customer get their outcome than being right**. You will most certainly experience moments when the customer is wrong and you know it. You may even be able to prove to the customer that you are right. And, you will have lost a customer.

Ultimately, regardless of who the customer is, a spouse, friend, child or business associate, the most valuable thing you can leave with them is a better state.

The only way this can happen consistently is if you take responsibility for making it happen.

The 4 Laws of Service

Chapter 8
LAW #4
ADD VALUE

Many people would assume that this should be the first law. That's what Customer Service is all about, added value right? Yes, and you and the customer both have to be in a resourceful state to make sure it is delivered properly.

I am going to assume that you already have a product or service that offers superior value. This chapter is about *how* to add value to the person. Ultimately, it is the quality of our relationships, not our products that bring joy to our lives.

Step #1
How May I Serve YOU?

This is the most important question to ask in service. The key part of this sentence is the YOU. The only way you can add value to someone is to give something *they* find valuable.

All to often we assume we know what is valuable to other people. Each and every person is an individual and they want to be treated that way. The more specific you can be in delivering value to your customers, the greater chance they will recognize and respond to that value.

As parents this means that you treat each child as an individual. One child may feel valued by receiving a gift. Another may just want to spend time. And the other may need to hear words of appreciation. Of course each of them will want all of these things over time, however each child has a strategy that will have the most impact on them. Find it, and use it.

Sherlock Holmes?

How do you discover what is valuable to someone? Ask. Pay attention. Get to know your customers. Do market research. Keep client files. ***These customers are your business.***

Amazon.com is one of the most successful companies on the Internet. They have created an entirely new market for book buyers. One of the keys to their success are their customer profiles. They keep an in-depth profile on each of their customers, that is then matched to their database of books. The client then receives a list of other books they may like based on their buying habits. ***That is creating specific value for the individual customer.***

Step #2
Exceed Customers Expectations

Customer Satisfaction Guaranteed. **A satisfied customer is a customer who is looking for a better price, value or service**. Satisfaction is not enough. There are many companies with satisfied customers that no longer exist. As we already have discussed, excellence is the minimum standard that people expect today. Their money and time is too valuable to waste on average. To stand out, to be world-class, you need to be outstanding in creating value for them. When customer's expectations are not just met, but exceeded on a consistent basis, they become raving fans. They tell people about you. They will give you repeat business. They will be loyal.

Exceeding is not just doing what you say. If you tell your son you are going to be at his ball game, and you are, you have met his expectation. You have a satisfied customer. If you miss the game, you have a very disappointed and hurt customer. If you are supposed to be out of town on business but you take an earlier flight home so you can make it to the game, you have exceeded expectations and you have a raving fan.

This does not mean that you never promise anything. It means that you under promise and over deliver. In the above example, you could exceed expectations by bringing a treat for the team, or picking up one of his grandparents on the way to the game. Here's an example;

Lexus has a well-deserved reputation for delivering outstanding service. My father has driven Lexus vehicles for several years now. He likes the cars, but he loves the service. It wasn't just the day he picked up his first Lexus. It's three cars later and occurs day in and day out.

Here is an example. He had the car at the dealership to fix one of the front headlights. As he was driving to the airport to leave on a business trip, his car phone rang. He picked it up and it was the service manager from the Lexus dealership.

Was he calling to see if the headlight was working? No. "Hi, Mr. Bagshaw. This is Joe with Lexus. I was just driving beside you and I noticed that the headlight still is not working properly. I would like to come buy and pick up the car at your office, and leave you with a replacement while we rework the computer to fix it."

"Thank you for the call", my Dad replied. "However I am on my way to the airport, so why don't we do it when I get back from my trip".

"Tell you what, let me know where you park the car, and I'll send someone to pick it up, and make sure it is fixed and waiting for you when you return", Joe replied.

That is exactly what happened. When my Dad returned from his trip, there was his car in the exact same stall and ready to go. Joe had a moment of truth. He was in a resourceful state, focused on "how may I serve?" and therefore exceeded the customer's expectations. He didn't have to call. No one would have known. It is this type of service that has made my father a raving fan.

Step #3
Make it Easy

Life is complicated enough. People don't want their "added value" to be added hassle.

There is a chain photo-finishing store that we purchased an "added value" discount card from. The idea is that you can use the card to get a discount on all of your purchases in the store. The first challenge is that you only get one card. So when my wife has the card, and I pick-up the film, I don't have the card. The second problem is, without the card I have to call a special number and request the discount be credited to me. This is not added value, this is added hassle.

There is a Hotel in Vancouver that understands the importance of added value. When you arrive at your room; there is a stack of personalized business cards waiting for you. They have your name, room telephone number and the dates you are staying. This is a simple idea that exceeds customer's expectations, is very specific to you and is made easy. As the customer you don't have to fill out forms or call in your request, you simply pick-up the cards and start using them.

It's the little things that count

Tomorrow on your way home, stop and pick up your partner's favorite treat and surprise them. Call in the middle of the afternoon just to tell them you love them. Bring home take-out for the kids unannounced. Take an afternoon off to go to the zoo. These are what Stephen Covey calls making deposits in the emotional bank account. When you are in service to people you are making deposits. When you are focused on your own agenda, you are likely making withdrawals.

Now you need to decide how you can use the 4 Laws of Service to create an abundance of what you truly want in your life.

Chapter 9
THRIVING ON CHANGE

Change is the greatest obstacle we face in our lives. Change often comes in many forms. From the obvious job loss or health crisis to the more subtle experience when some of life's challenges leave us alone for a while. Every new experience, good or bad, is change.

Change is often seen as that "thing" which is preventing us from doing our work. In the global economy of the 21st Century learning to thrive on change is our work, it is not the block in the road but the road itself.

Probably the single most important skill anyone can learn is the ability to adapt to change. There is nothing more vital in the 21st century than this skill. I know many people have made the argument that the key skill is technology, or people skills. While these are valuable tools, if you are unable to adapt to the constantly changing world, all other skills will be useless because you will not have the opportunity to apply them.

Part of the challenge in adapting to change is that it is seen only as the big obstacles. The companies' merger. A divorce. Moving to a new city. It is critical to understand that as a culture we are facing changes everyday. The growth of our children put us face to face with change with every new phase. Our intimate relationships are constantly fluctuating, not to mention what is happening with the world as a whole.

Like all skills, adapting to change can be learned with practice. Once the core organizing principle has been developed, you can begin to see change for what it really is, an opportunity. As the old saying goes, for every seed of adversity there is an equal or greater opportunity for success. It is when we truly *know* the truth of that statement that we can begin to *thrive on change.*

The Comfort Zone

The comfort zone is the area in our lives where we feel emotionally secure. It is a wall we construct around us to protect ourselves. Once the circumstances of our lives take us beyond that imaginary wall, we begin to become unbalanced. Each of us has a different comfort zone and therefore a different response when the challenges of life force us outside of it. Often, many of the rewards we want in our life require us to expand our comfort zone beyond its current limits. A promotion, a new relationship or increased health may be a few of the things we are striving for beyond the wall of our current comfort zone.

Challenge or opportunity, we must all continue to grow and expand or we will shrink and die.

Thriving on change is the ability to thrive regardless of the challenge. Many highly successful business people can handle the thrill and uncertainty of making a deal or starting a new venture. They feel the incredible high and feed off the energy that creates. For them, the challenge is when the excitement is gone. They crash. The adrenaline rush is over and they desperately search for the next challenge.

For others, the challenge is in facing new opportunities. Unlike the above example, they fear the unknown. They function fine when their life is predictable and secure. The moment that is taken away, they begin to shut down. Stress, anger, frustration and depression are just a few of the emotions they may experience.

FEAR

The biggest obstacle most of us must overcome in our lives is fear. Fear builds the wall that traps us inside of our comfort zone. Everyone has different fears. Fear of failure, success, rejection, loss, change, the list goes on and on. Unchecked, a fear will continue to grow until it literally can run your life. At the very least, it will continually prevent you from rising to the challenges of life and fulfilling your potential.

This does not mean that fear is necessarily a bad thing. When recognized for what it is, a call to action, the incredible amount of energy that fear generates can be used to break through the fear. Unfortunately, most people take that energy and turn it into worry, doubt and stress.

The greatest antidote for fear is faith. Faith is the key that will allow you to handle any challenge and overcome any amount of change.

The Most Valuable State

As soon as I mention Faith, most people assume I am about to get religious on them. It is certainly true that many people find their greatest source of faith from their religious beliefs. However this is not the only source of faith. In fact, people who build their faith based on external sources (relationships, their company, friends the economy) are almost certainly going to face a major crisis of faith at some point in their lives.

Faith is an internal experience. Faith is a choice. Like a seed, it must be nurtured in order to grow. As children we seem to have an unlimited amount of faith, probably because we have not yet severed the connection to that part of us that is changeless. However, like a garden, if left unattended it can wither and die. The good news is that we can always plant a new garden.

Once you have developed a strong foundation of faith, you can begin to utilize the most important tool in Thriving on Change, Emotional Certainty.

Emotional Certainty

Our daughter was about 3 months old and Lipi and I had taken the summer off to spend it with our beautiful blessing. Through a series of "co-incidences" we had a meeting with the CEO of an international seminar company. We ended up being offered the opportunity to represent this company, and the speaker whose work the company was based on, exclusively in Canada.

We went down to their headquarters to start the process. This was early October. We moved out of our current condo to an acreage so that we would have the amount of space needed to build this company. The first order of business was to set up a tour for the speaker to generate increased awareness.

It was right at this time that I woke up one morning and turned to Lipi and said, " I think we're going to have another baby."

"You know what, I think you're right", she replied with her wonderful smile. So off to the pharmacy I went to get a home pregnancy test. Indeed our wonderful little boy was on his way.

We continued to prepare for our new business. We developed business plans, created the logo and all the stationary and began to research strategic alliances to distribute all of the products across the country.

November passed, nothing confirmed.

December passed; we were assured everything would be finalized after the holidays.

About mid-January we were informed that the CEO we had made the deal with was no longer with the company. The Canadian rights that we had discussed were no longer available.

What now? We had already invested several months into the project and now it looked like there would be no return at all. We had an 8-month old daughter and another child coming in 5 months.

***Everything happens for a reason and a purpose and it serves me, if I choose it to** kept ringing in my head. This was a belief that had served us well over the past few years. We knew that there had to be a reason why it was falling apart. We just didn't know what. So after several meditations and brain storming sessions, we came up with a list of alternatives. The best option was to use our contact and the leverage of the broken agreement to arrange for the primary speaker to come and do a couple of lectures and perhaps a weekend program in Canada.*

It would be a win-win for both sides. They would get their speaking fee and first class exposure in our market, we would get the opportunity to deliver a world class experience to our clients and generate reasonable return on our investment.

We presented our proposal to our original contact. Even though he sincerely wanted to assist us, he felt there was no way that our request could be accommodated. The person responsible for booking the seminars had a reputation for being "difficult".

Crisis. Nothing was going as planned. What to do? Where to go? Get a job? We believed that this was the project we should be working on.

As we wrestled with the sheer frustration of our situation, we knew that we would **never be given more than we could handle.** *Life is a series of challenges. Like the tree in a storm, if we are brittle and are always resisting the inevitable changes going on around us, we will snap like a twig. On the other had, if we view this storm as an opportunity to grow and become stronger, we will be flexible enough to bend in the wind and see the glorious sunshine that follows every storm.*

One of the ways we progress in life is through lessons. We will continue to get the same lessons until we learn them. After a lengthy discussion with our good friend Brandon Bays, we realized that we were playing out our self-worth lesson. This had come up time and time again. This was the principle lesson we thought we had learned in the earlier situation with a business partner.

It was time to stand up for the value we had to offer. We had to stop waiting for the opportunity to just "show up". We called our contact and suggested that we would get our lawyers involved if we were not given the opportunity to promote the seminars in our market that spring.

Finally, we secured two lectures for the spring. One in Edmonton, one in Calgary. Based on detailed discussions with their Director of seminars, we also elected to hold a weekend workshop in the summer, after the birth of our son.

The window of opportunity was small. We had only 8 weeks until the lectures. We had to put together the entire marketing plan, secure venues, get media sponsors and of course sell tickets.

We leveraged our time, energy and capital to put together an outstanding marketing package. The last time this speaker had been in Edmonton, he had only drawn 300 people. Our target was 2000. In Calgary the target was a sell out at 1800.

The idea was to have people come to the lecture and then give them the opportunity to enroll into the weekend workshop. We had been told that historically they had a 10% rollover from the lectures into the weekend program. Based on those figures we felt we could put 400+ people into the weekend event, assuming we hit our lecture targets.

That is exactly what we did. Calgary was sold-out nearly a week in advance and Edmonton ended up with over 2300 people. A massive success with a total of over 4100 attendees, two of the largest lectures they had all year. We got along wonderfully with the speaker and our clients were very happy.

One small problem, there was not a 10% enrollment into the weekend. There were only about 20 people total, in both cities. We discussed this with the marketing director, and she reassured us that most of the enrollments would come from our follow-up marketing piece.

So we went out with our direct mail piece, and continued to do other media advertising as well. We were extremely optimistic about the weekend event. We had created such a stir with the marketing of the lectures; we might even be able to get 450-500 into the weekend.

A Curve ball

Lipi was now 8 months pregnant. An ultra sound revealed she had a rare condition called vasa-prevea. The baby was fine, however this meant the baby could not be delivered vaginally. If she went into labor, she could bleed to death and the baby would drown in the blood within a couple of minutes. This meant the baby would have to be taken early by C-section and the 45-minute drive to the nearest hospital could prove to be an extreme challenge.

What was interesting, was that our initial reaction was one of ***gratefulness****. Grateful that the baby was okay, and that the condition was discovered. Lipi's sister is a radiologist and she told us that they usually don't discover this condition until the woman is in labor, and then it is a life and death situation.*

We realized there was absolutely no use in getting upset or worried. Everything is either going to work out, or we are going to have a challenge that will effect us for the rest of our lives. If everything works out, then our worry would have been wasted. If there were complications, then why would we want to waste even a single precious moment being stressed? Life was much, much too precious to be wasted on what might happen. All of lifes joy is experienced in the present moment. Fear cannot exist in the present moment. It certainly wasn't easy, but we knew that we must live in the now for the sake of our unborn child, and the child we had with us.

There is only one thing in the entire universe that we have any control over, our own state.

When life throws you a curve ball, you need to de-

velop a strategy for hitting it. That's what we did. We went out and found a nanny/assistant. The idea was for her to help out in the office, with the house-work and in caring for Kennedy, who was now 11 months old.

We continued to market the program. Sales were going well, however certainly not where we wanted them to be.

We felt the early bird registration cut off would be give us a very good indication of what our sales would be. The organization told us they have about 95% of their enrollments by this cut-off.

With two weeks to the cut-off, we hit another obstacle. Our nanny/assistant decided this wasn't what she was looking for. She decided to leave. Is this ever going to end? One thing after another. If challenges make you stronger, I felt like I was about to break.

Finally it was time to take off the brave face we had put on for our families and admit that we needed help. We had prided ourselves on being self -sufficient and being able to handle whatever came up. We finally realized we had not been utilizing one of our greatest resources, our family. Often the help we need is right in front of us, a friend, family, a co-worker; we just have to ask for it.

The countdown was on. Sales sucked and the doctor ordered Lipi into the hospital for complete bed rest. If all went well they would take the baby in a week. If the baby was not ready, two weeks.

I spent the next two weeks driving the two hour round trip to the hospital at least once a day. Every moment was shifting from my concern for Lipi, to generating as many sales as possible to spending every available moment with my one-year-old daughter. To cope with this massive project, Lipi had the Laptop in the hospital with her and was processing orders in her bed.

Christian was born in perfect health. Lipi and I rejoiced at the miracle of life. We cherished the first few days we had alone with him in the hospital. Even though Kennedy was only one, she was very excited about the new addition to the family.

Reality Check

The early bird deadline had come and gone and we weren't even half way
to our goal of 400. Anything less than 300 would be a financial disaster. Once again here I was, a new child and the immediate future was not looking bright.

We were one month away from the event and the organization suggested we cut our losses by discontinuing our marketing efforts. 200 was a very respectable number. In fact it was their average for that year.

Fortunately we did not listen. We continued with our original plan. Lipi and I would switch between working in the office, taking registrations and caring for the children. As is the case with most parents of newborns, we were averaging 3-4 hours of sleep a day.

About 10 days out from the event we were at 300, respectable, but well short of our target. During a "where did we go wrong" conversation with the organizations Director of seminars, Lipi discovered that they in fact did not have accurate statistics about the number of people who enroll from the lecture into the weekend event, and it was likely closer to 3%, exactly what we had.

How could this be? We had done everything right. We were in shock. Our entire marketing plan was based on those stats. We would have marketed the event totally different if we had had the proper information. We had to get to the bottom of this.

It was right at this time that the final and largest chunk of the speaker's fee was due. Should we pay or not. That little tidbit of missing information was going to cost us tens of thousands of dollars in lost revenue. This wasn't right.

We suggested that we would not pay the remainder of the fee until the matter could be resolved. The organization response was that we had a contract and that unless they received their money, they would pull the speaker out of the event. We, of course, felt the contract may be void because the information we used to enter into the agreement was inaccurate.

The Greatest Source of Strength

At this point, there was only one place I could turn for guidance. I went for a walk on the 4 acres surrounding our home. I found a quiet place and kneeled down. I offered up a sincere prayer for how grateful I was for my beautiful, healthy family.

I then asked what should we do? What was the right thing? How could we honor the greatness of everyone involved? I got a calm, warm feeling all over my body. I had a sense of absolute certainty and a knowing, ***if I do my best and do what is right, I will always be taken care of.***

We had done our best. We were doing what we believed to be the right course of action. We would not pay the money until we could resolve this matter.

The speaker arrived in Calgary as planned. Although we had not slept in three days, the set up for the event went smoothly.

On the morning of the first day, approximately one

hour before the first session was about to begin, the assistant facilitator pulled Lipi aside and indicated to her that they were going to pull out of the event if they did not receive their money immediately.

I had learned years earlier that, "Its in your moments of decision that your destiny is shaped". This was certainly a destiny shaping moment, a moment of truth. Not pay the money and risk having to cancel an event and give out over $100,000 in refunds, or pay the money and go against our principles of what is right and wrong.

In a moment I decided not to pay. They were not right. It hadn't been resolved. In that moment I experienced the raw emotions I am sure the ancient warriors lived daily, the exhilaration of standing up for what I believed and the heart stopping panic that I could be destroyed at any moment. Whatever the result, I had the knowing that ***I was in complete control of my Destiny and I was being true to myself.***

What's my Outcome?

The cause had been set in motion. All I could do now was prepare for the effect. What was my outcome? Give our clients an outstanding weekend. They had paid $395 each, some traveling a great distance to attend this workshop. No matter what happened, we had to deliver a world-class experience to these people. So, we carried on as if the event was going ahead as scheduled.

Later that afternoon I met with the "speaker" and we came to an understanding. He delivered a world-class outstanding weekend. Our clients were thrilled. We enjoyed a well-deserved rest.

"For any of us to be truly free-
If we are to learn to soar in this changing
world we must first be willing to
be responsible for our lives."
- David McNally

Thriving on change is a skill. Change comes at us from all directions. Personal, business, health, relationships, technology, the list goes on. Emotional certainty is created by having a belief system that focuses you in the direction of your goals, not in the direction of your obstacles.

It is when we are thriving on change that we can bring the best of ourselves forward to each new challenge, and therefore be of increasing value to those we serve.

Chapter 10
CREATING CERTAINTY IN A MOMENT

Emotional certainty is a choice, not a reward. Certainty (absolute confidence) does not come with a 6-figure income or the next promotion. It is created internally on a moment-to-moment basis. It is a state; a highly productive state that allows you to tap into the greatness that is at the core of who you really are.

Certainty is the state where you know anything is possible. It is the Rocky Balboa inside each of us that knows we can rise to the occasion and be the best we can be.

Step #1
Present Moment

The first step is to be in the present moment. The greatest enemy of certainty is fear. Fear cannot exist in the present moment. Do not get caught up in the past and don't waist your energy worrying about the future.

Take a deep breath in and exhale. While you are doing it, only pay attention to your breath… That was the present moment. Be here, now. There is no quick way to learning how to be in the present moment. Monks in the Buddhist tradition spend a lifetime of practice learning how to *be in the moment.*

Think of a time when you were competing in an athletic event. What was your performance like if you were thinking about your stack of papers back at the office? Probably not so hot. The same is true when you encounter any challenge. Look at it like a competition. Not with the other people around you, but with yourself to be the best you can be.

Sometimes your best will be an aggressive warrior like state. Ready to take massive action. Sometimes however it may need to be a nurturing caregiver state. Remember, flexibility is power.

Step #2
The best way to prepare for an uncertain future is to create the on you want

Certainty and courage are very similar emotions. When we think of people who have courage, we often think of people like Rosa Parks taking that fateful trip on the bus in the Deep South that sparked a revolution. Or Nelson Mandela spending a lifetime in prison waiting for the opportunity to lead his people and his country to freedom.

Courage comes from having a vision of the future. A reason to dig down deep and bring out the best of ourselves. To do what is not easy to do. To keep going while others have given up. We must have an inspired vision of what you want and who you must become to achieve it.

Creating an Inspired Vision

1. ***Create an Inspired state.*** Before you create your Inspired Vision, you need to be in a state were you can access your greatness. I usually spend a couple of days to create a truly inspired state. I will often watch a movie like Braveheart or Schindlers List. Movies like these touch my heart and allow me to open up to what really has meaning in my life. I may also go for a walk along the river behind our home. Communing with nature has a wonderful way of settling the mind and uplifting the soul. Occasionally I will even fast for twenty-four hours. Fasting clears the mind and body and heightens spiritual awareness. As I begin the process I will light a candle and put on some of my favorite music.

2. ***Think Possibility:*** If anything were possible, what would your Inspired Destiny be. It is essential that you create a vision for your life that gets you up in the morning, what is called a healthy obsession. At the end of your life, what has to happen for you to be proud of your time on this planet? What do you believe in? Who will you become?

   Think of any individual who has achieved greatness and added value to humanity. They all held an Inspired Vision for their life. Gandhi, Martin Luther King Jr., Walt Disney, Mother Theresa. We are all much better off for their visions.

Ask yourself the question "What would happen if I..."?

3. ***Think Realistically.*** Most people over estimate what they can accomplish in a year, and under estimate what they can do in a decade. The idea is to create a realistic plan without dampening your vision. The realistic part is not the vision, but the timeline. As you plan out your action steps and benchmarks, be realistic.
   Ask yourself "what can I realistically expect to accomplish in X period of time" Now create a time line with action steps.

4. ***Take action.*** Just as Nike says, Just Do It.

5. ***Evaluate and improve.*** Are your actions taking you in the direction of your vision? If yes, continue. If not, try a new approach.

Now that you have your vision, use it to access your courage in the moment.

Step #3
Physiology of Certainty

Like any other state, certainty has a physiology. Stand or sit up straight, head up, eyes looking straight ahead. Creating a feeling of invincibility in your body.

Create a recipe for the state of certainty. Think of the times in your life when you have felt certain. Go back to one of those times right now. How were you standing?

Breathing? What were you focusing on? Make a list and practice recreating this state as often as you can so it becomes natural to you.

It is often valuable to "pick a hero" and model how they create certainty. As an example, I like to use Mel Gibson's character in BraveHeart, William Wallace, as an example of certainty. When I am in need of courage I ask myself, "What would William Wallace do right know"? This helps me to take the actions I need to.

You can use this technique for any state. I will also use other people whom I admire such as Jesus Christ, Gandhi, or John F. Kennedy.

This is not about trying to be someone else. We all share the same essential physiology, so if Gandhi created a certain state by moving his body in a specific fashion, and if I do the same thing, I will experience similar emotions. This technique is especially useful when I work with professional athletes and have them model themselves when they are at their best.

Step #4
Take Action

Directed action. If it's wrong, learn from it, develop a new plan and once again, take action. Indecisiveness comes from sitting around weighing your options. Put yourself in a resourceful state and take action. Pay attention to see if you get the result you want. Compare your result to the future you want to create for yourself. If you are on course, keep doing it. If not, change your approach, and keep changing it until you get what you want.

THRIVING ON CHANGE

DAILY RITUAL

Just like any other skill, thriving on change must be conditioned over time. The following are 5 steps that you can do everyday to condition yourself.

Step #1
Clear the Mind

Meditation is a wonderful tool for living from the Inside-Out. It allows your mind the opportunity to settle and your consciousness to dip into the infinite intelligence of the universe.

There are many techniques for meditating. You can get a book or take a course. Or you can just simply do the following:

- sit in a comfortable position, keeping your spine as straight as possible,
- close your eyes and focus your attention on your breath. Just notice your breath as it comes in and as it goes out.
- When thoughts come into your mind, just let them go. Don't try and make them go away, this will only make them stronger, just let them pass across the screen in your mind. Then bring your attention back to your breath.

That is meditating. Do that for 10-20 minutes twice a day and the results will be profound. The longer and more regularly you do it, the better the results. Ideally you will do it first thing in the morning and at the end of your work-day.

Step #2
Focus the Camera

Questions are the best tool for focusing your camera. Put 4 or 5 questions on a cue card by your bed or put it on the mirror where you get ready in the morning. As you get ready, ask your self the questions. This will prime your mind for the day and help you to get into the appropriate state for the challenges ahead.

Here are a few sample questions:

- What am I most excited about today?
- What state must I be in today to have an outstanding day?
- How may I serve?
- What's great about today?
- What would happen if I...today?

Step #3
Fill up the Emotions

The most valuable emotion is that of being grateful. Nothing fills up an empty emotional tank like being grateful. So take a few minutes and write down 4-5 things you are most grateful for in your life. Your family, your health, the fact that you have a job to go to even if you don't like it. The birds are singing in the tree or the fact that you having running water to take your shower with.

If you are having trouble "being grateful" ask yourself, "If I *was* grateful for something, what would it be?"

There is no way that you can create a Constantly Increasing Quality of Life if you are not grateful for what you already have. The abundance of the universe is attracted to gratefulness. If you want more, be grateful for what you have. And the beauty of it is, the more you are grateful for what you have, the less attached you are to things you do not have.

Step #4
Flexibility is Power

There is a great deal of research that shows us the mind and body are connected at the deepest level. What occurs in the mind, occurs in the body. And what occurs in the body occurs in the mind.

This means that to have a flexible mind, you must have a flexible body. Yoga is an excellent tool for creating flexibility in both mind and body.

Once again there are many excellent books and courses on yoga. The best yoga teachers I have had have taught that it's not the specific stretch that makes the difference but the awareness that you bring to the movement.

As you stretch, pay attention to the movement and breath. The breath is the most important part. Even 5 minutes of mindful stretching can help to increase your flexibility. You can do it in the morning or even while you are sitting at your desk. The important thing is to do it.

"A little bit of something is better than a lot of nothing."
Dan Millman

Step #5
Go to the Mind Gym

To condition any muscle you must workout on a regular basis. The same is true of your mind. Read self-help books or inspirational literature. Listen to books on tape in your car or on your Walkman while you workout. Take a course. Review your inspiring vision. Write in your journal. Whatever it is, do it daily.

These five steps are just a guideline to creating the optimal state on the ***Inside*** so that you can produce outstanding results on the ***Outside***. They should only take 20-30 minutes in the morning and will create a significant return on your investment of time and energy.

"It is our very search for perfection outside
ourselves that causes our suffering."
Buddha

Chapter 11
TRANSFORMATIONAL LEADERSHIP

"Your first and foremost job as a leader is to take charge of your own energy and then help to orchestrate the energy of those around you."

Peter Drucker, professor, author and leading authority on economics, management and leadership.

The greatest examples we have of outstanding service have not come from organizations, products or even The Local Order of Water Buffalo. The greatest examples we have are the result of a select group of individuals making a decision to make a difference.

Individuals who took it upon themselves to make a difference have significantly impacted the course of human history. In the 20th century it has been people like Martin Luther King Jr., Gandhi, John F. Kennedy and Mother Teresa to name a few. All of these people have one thing in common; they lead a life of service. They had very different ways of expressing their desire to serve, but never the less they have all made a lasting impact on our world.

In studying the lives of these amazing people, I noticed there were many similarities in the way they achieved their objectives. They lead many people, often, entire countries in a new direction. They helped to shift the consciousness of this planet. Yet, they did not worry about the corporate culture or whether the corporate policies have been put in place to take care of the customer. They lead by example and they lead by purpose. They inspired others to greatness.

Engage their Hearts

What makes the transformational leader so powerful? They tap into the greatest resource their people have; they engage their hearts. The transformational leader captures the imagination and shows her people how they and those around them will become better by making the vision a reality. When a person's heart is engaged, he or she becomes a willing participant. Without it, they are simply being obedient.

Some say it was their destiny. Maybe it was. Just like you are destined for greatness in your own life. The difference between this group of people and the average person is the average person waits, while the transformational leader acts.

There are four common traits that all servant leaders share. They are not mystical or inborn. They are skills. For some they were learned over a lifetime. For others, they were awakened by the pain of injustice. Either way, you also have these skills waiting to be unlocked.

People do not follow a title,
They follow passion,
they follow certainty
They follow vision.

#1
Know Your Outcome

Simple, yet profound. The power of intention is the one of the most powerful forces in the universe. Nothing is created until it is an intention. Every action is proceeded by a thought. A thought is an intention.

The clearer and more concise you are on your outcome, the more likely you are to achieve it. Your mind is like a homing device. When you give it an accurate target, it sets out to find it.

When Gandhi was thrown off the train in South Africa because he did not have the right pigmentation in his skin, he become very clear on his outcome. As he lead his followers against the British Empire in a stand of Non-violence, he wasn't thinking in the back of his head, "If this doesn't work maybe we can get our hands on a nuclear bomb". He was absolutely clear on what is outcome was and he kept his eye on the "ball" no matter how hard it got.

It is this clarity that creates incredible power. There is no second-guessing, no doubt. Martin Luther King Jr. did not stand up and inspire people by saying " I have a Strategic Plan!". No, he had a Dream and he believed it was possible. His belief was so powerful that it transcended race and to this day many people are brought to tears when they hear this speech.

What is your Outcome?

What is the vision for your life? What are you going to give the vast energy of your existence to? How can you generate more passion and more certainty about your vision right now. As we learned earlier, you can only share what you have.

#2
Leverage

"Give me a lever long enough and
I can single handily move the world."
- Archimedes

Leverage is creating a greater return on your investment of time energy and capital than you expend. This is an obvious principle that is used to build a successful business and investment portfolio. It should also be used to be an outstanding leader of people.

Jesus profoundly taught this principle, "Give a man a fish, you feed him for a day. Teach a man how to fish, you feed him for a life time". This is the essence of leverage. The following is a story of a saint who understood the power of leverage.

An invading army had attacked a village and the local army troops had been defeated. The survivors had been imprisoned. One of the local businessmen heard that the troops did not have any clean water. So he went to the warden of the prison camp and requested the opportunity to provide clean water to the prisoners. Knowing that without clean water the prisoners would become ill and be much more difficult to care for, the warden granted the request.

A few days later another well-intentioned businessman discovered that the prisoners were sleeping on the cold, dirt floors. He approached the warden and offered to provide blankets for the prisoners to sleep on. Again the warden understood the value of well-rested "workers" for rebuilding the village.

Another local businessman discovered the prisoners did not have proper food. He went to the warden and offered to provide the prisoners with fresh food. Understanding that hungry men were rebellious men, he granted the request.

Finally, the saint happened across the village. He saw what was happening. He went to the prison camp and found the keys, and let all of the prisoners go.

All of the other men were very well intentioned, however their actions did not solve the problem they only made it more comfortable.

In creating leverage, the key question to ask yourself is, What ***will create the greatest amount of happiness for the largest number of people over the longest period of time?***

Once you have answered this question, make it happen.

#3
Honor The Greatness

The Greatness in Me
Honors the Greatness in You

NAMASTE

There is a place where we are all equal. A place were position, gender or race are irrelevant. Deep inside each of us we know this. All you have to do is look at a newborn baby and you will recognize the miracle that we all came from.

Outstanding leaders see the greatness in each of us as individuals, as well as a group. On of the greatest examples in modern history was the inaugural speech of John F. Kennedy.

"People of America, Ask not what your country can do for you, but ask what you can do for your country. Citizens of the world, ask not what America can do for you but ask what we can do together for the freedom of man."

Kennedy is considered one of the greatest leaders in modern history because he stirred that greatness that resides inside each and every one of us. Like all transformational leaders, he appealed to our sense of service. He understood that inherently we all know our purpose is to serve. He held us to the highest standard, the standard we often fail to hold ourselves to.

4 Keys to Honoring the Greatness in Others

1. ***Be respectful***. Treat each person as the miracle that they really are, even though their current behavior may indicate otherwise.

2. ***Talk to their greatness***. When you communicate to someone, talk to the part of them that knows anything is possible. Do not get caught up in a battle with their ego over who has had the worst day.

3. ***Choose kindness***. In any moment there is any number of ways a given situation can be handled, whenever possible, take a deep breath and choose kindness.

4. ***Hold people to a higher standard***. The greatest coaches

are not those who can play the game the best. They are those who can bring the best game out of their players.

#4
Act AS If...

"In order to be a great champion you must believe that you are the best...and if you are not, pretend that you are."
Muhammad Ali

Martin Luther King Jr. did not wait to see his dream of racial equality become a reality before he began to act as if it were already true. Nor did Mother Theresa wait to be recognized for her kindness. Arnold saw himself as Mr. Universe and a great film star with every weight he pumped. These individuals and anyone else who has risen to greatness in their life understood the importance of becoming the person you want to be on the inside before it can be realized in the outside world.

You don't suddenly become confident because you are successful; you become successful because you are confident.

Who do you want to be?

Once you are clear on your what you want to create in your life, you can determine who you need to be to make it a reality. If you want to be a great leader, make a list of all the traits a great leader would have. If your calling is to be a parent to your children, what are all the traits of an outstanding parent? You get the idea?

Make the list as detailed as possible. Several years ago I used this exercise to create my ideal relationship. I sat down and made a detailed description of what my ideal relationship would be and from that what my ideal partner would be like. Once I knew what I wanted, I made a list of the traits I would need to have to be able to create this relationship in my life. Once I had the list I immediately began to act as if I already had these traits. In other words, I began to practice these traits every single day. I am happy to report that I was able to attract the love of my life, my wife Lipi, shortly after I began this practice.

Now the first thing I often hear when I suggest this idea is that you are not being genuine when you take this approach. You really aren't that person so how dare you walk around pretending to be someone you are not. Well, I am not suggesting you go to the hospital and put on the white jacket and start doing rounds if you are not a doctor. However, if you want to become a doctor, what would happen if you identified some of the key traits of outstanding doctors and began to develop them for yourself? This is called modeling and is used by virtually all successful people.

Chapter 12 Create a Living Legacy

The only thing hat we have for sure is this moment, right here right now. Many people talk about the importance of leaving a legacy. They suggest you imagine you are at your 80th birthday and reflect on your life. Or imagine you are at your funeral write your own eulogy. Of the course the purpose of these exercises is to help you get clear on the legacy that you want to leave. They are very powerful exercises that I have used myself.

The challenge I have for you is to bring this concept to today. If today were your last day, what would your legacy be? And not only the legacy of your entire life (i.e. your children, your career, your contributions) but the legacy of today. If your life were to be measured by your actions on a single day, how would you be measured…today?

Be a person who makes a positive meaningful impact on the people you meet everyday. Be a person who leaves such a mark on someone that they talk about you at the dinner table.

"How was your day dear?"

"You know, it was really great. I had a meeting with this amazing person (your name). He/she was so full of life. I was having a pretty rough day but after our meeting, the day just went great."

You are the director of your movie. Design the character to make it the most successful, enjoyable movie ever. The more you are enjoying your own movie, the better your supporting cast will enjoy it.

You have been given an incredible gift, its called life. With all its challenges, ups and downs and lessons, it is an amazing gift. Use it wisely. You have the power to make an incredible impact on the people you come in contact with. The greatest lives are the lives lived in the service of others. It is in service that we find joy, happiness, and challenge. The juice of life.

Make your life a blockbuster.

"The enjoyment of life's gifts constitutes living, not the number of days we are given to live."
Buddhist saying

Who must I become?

- Writer
- vision
- outcome
  - ↳ What do you want to ~~create~~ creat

Result
↑
Action
↑
State

- Improve memory
- manage the stress
-

What are the action step.

- Read about it
- See a specialist
- Practice
-

- relax/Breath
- Exercise
- take on smaller activities
- Do something for self 1st
- proper diet

~~What are~~
Who do you need to become

- confident about abilities
- Believe it can be done
  & Do it
- make the time
- Believe momentum

Focus

* write down before you sleep
you outcome for the next day.
eg - outstanding leader
- everyone to have a
wonderful day

sub
conscious
88%
12
conscious

Praise for Darren Bagshaw

"Darren, what can I say about the actual delivery of the course, it was nothing short of brilliant. I have to say it was the most phenomenal training experience I have ever had the pleasure of participating in. The course was rated as a 10 on a scale of 1-7".

E.J. (Lyn) Taylor, Vice-President
Personal & Wealth Markets, Royal Bank of Canada

"The reason I continue to send my clients to Darren Bagshaw is to give these professional athletes, including the #1 NHL Draft Pick for 1999, the competitive edge. ...Darren is absolutely outstanding at what he does!"

Rich Winter, CEO, The Sports Corporation

"One of the best decisions I have made as a leader was to invite you to conduct a day long seminar for my senior leaders... Thank you for assisting us in creating a team that is positively focused on meeting very challenging goals with a passion we haven't experienced before."

Gordon H. Oliver, Vice-President,
B.C. Interior, Bank of Montreal

"Simply Outstanding! Darren's high energy and ability to capture the groups attention was phenomenal. We have previously experienced numerous group sessions with our branch managers however your Personal Leadership session was 'Simply the Best'. "

Bev Voice, Senior Vice-President
B.C. & Yukon, Scotiabank

"Darren conducted one of their seminars for myself and my management team and the unanimous verdict was "TERRIFIC"!"

Les Pyette, Publisher & CEO , The Calgary Sun

"The boardbreaking was a brilliant finale, and I believe added value to individuals' personal as well as workplace lives."

Neal Hamblin, Vice-President
President's Choice Financial